The source

How to Realize Your Super Power!

DR. UNDRAI FIZER

DIVINE **[DH]** HOUSE

B O O K S

ISBN: 979-889660434-1

TABLE OF CONTENTS

HOW IT BEGINS...

"Wherever our LOVE and DESIRES reside, our greatest Strength, Joy, and Power will be REVEALED!" –Undrai F. Fizer

"I live where I need to. I live where I find Joy! I do not consider my Path to be dangerous, or different. It's where my JOY is. I have seized the place of my passion. If my passion seems to be far away to You, it's because it wasn't meant to be seized by You!"-Undrai F. Fizer

"The love of work is the secret to personal progress, productivity, and fulfillment because work encourages the release of potential, and potential is the abundance of talents, abilities, and capabilities given to every person." – Myles Munroe

"Good management of bad experiences, lead to personal growth!" –John Maxwell

"If you are not living in Joy, you are out of integrity with your Soul." -Michael Beckwith

I personally enjoy calling our greatest version of Self, Creativity and Potential, and Ultimate Fulfillment of Purpose and Life; *A SUPERPOWER!* So, when you encounter this word throughout this book, you will know exactly where I'm coming from.

CHAPTER ONE
*Identifying The Space Where My Passions
Come Alive!*

Amid a world so full of calamities, chaos, and confusion, I have realized (and so have you), a Truth that is irrefutable; OUR GREATEST CONTRIBUTIONS ARE FOUND WHERE OUR DESIRE AND LOVE ARE RESONATING!

My Greatest Capacity and Ability. My Ultimate Joy. My Greatest Power and Strength. My Extreme Focus and Attention. My Treasures and Wit. My Wealth. My Heart and Soul. My reality in Everything, resonates in that Realm where the Source of My LOVE, resides.

It's impossible to perform with excellence, with *"anything"* the heart is not in. The only thing we can do is plan for toleration, average, and a *"somewhat, self-made satisfaction"* of a below standard attempt at something. We will settle for *"D's"* in subjects we despise. We will plan to complete *"at least half,"* of subjects we despise, and we will somehow *"manipulate our Consciousness to legalize it as a passing grade"* within our own minds.

It appears as though we exist continually within a *"loveless environment of Life."* If so, this is such a tragic reality of living and being. It appears that the best we can do *is "settle for average"* and *"the least,"* as it relates to RELATIONSHIP; FRIENDSHIP; CAREER; and even SPIRITUALITY! How sad is this?

NOTHING NEW UNDER THE SUN?

Solomon said in the Scriptures, *"The thing that hath been, it is that which shall be; and that which is done is that which shall be done, and there is no new thing under the sun*; **Ecclesiastes 1:9 KJV.**

An existence, thriving within a reality absent of Passion and Purpose, will naturally establish cycles of confusion, tolerance, and anxiety. They too, will begin to perceive life as the "once, great King Solomon" did when he forgot the divine love of his life, and settled for mere companionships with a myriad of relationships and companionships. Everything recycles itself where Conviction is absent. There remains nothing new to look forward to. Nothing exciting that will totally arrest the heart and navigate it to the Mysterious Powers of the Divine Knowing. The *Now Source* of

ALIVENESS and BEINGNESS! Same sun, same everything. A different day of the same NOTHINGNESS

Wherever TRUE LOVE resides.

I cannot tell you the meaning of LOVE, per se. The definition is realized within your own soul, body, and strength. LOVE is different to so many and can be realized through a myriad of feelings and sensations. You may like a *"love or feeling"* that weakens you and causes you to miss work in the morning. You may like a *"love or feeling"* that feels abusive and devaluing of your very being. You may like a *"love or a feeling"* that steals all your finances out of the bank. You may like a *"love or a feeling"* that takes advantage of your companionship, leaves you pregnant and with child, and then starts a new life with your best friend. Maybe LOVE to you, is finally being noticed and paid attention to. Maybe LOVE to you is being used and knowing it. Yet, the attention alone is attraction because you've never experienced the feelings of being paid attention to!

Souls, *that were once held hostage to invisibility*, loves the light that comes *from finally being "seen!"*

5

What can you tell a hungry soul that's yearning for the feelings of an experience that they feel they've been robbed of their entire life? Clarity is undesired, especially when the heart feels good being fooled! Wherever unconscious DYSFUNCTION resides, destruction will too. It's a sad thing to be sick and not know it.

To another, LOVE is loving the idea of being accepted by someone. It could be the joys of having someone else *"validating and approving"* your presence of Humanity. It could be someone else innately making you feel that your presence is worthy to exist in this world. And for that, YOU WILL DO ANYTHING TO PLEASE THEM *"while hoping that they will live to continue to remind YOU OF YOUR WORTHINES!"*

I cannot define for YOU *"what you desire to seek, for YOU!"* I will do nothing but disappoint your existence. My TRUTH may not be the Source of TRUTH you seek for YOU. And we cannot manipulate PRINCIPLE to serve as TRUTH for us. We are simply going to settle for what our heart is seeking after. And that's where the confusion lies. Our hurt and pain will determine how far we go in Clarity, or how much we can tolerate amid dissatisfaction. It's all up to what we can innately put up with within ourselves.

If your "greatest attribute" is a reality full of limitations, who would be the individual to reveal that it is a *"limitation?"* To YOU, that reality may be the best YOU see within yourself! That is why COMPARISON IS A THIEF TO JOY, especially when it is YOU *"who's guilty of the comparing!"* If YOU are full indeed, why would YOU *"look over your fence into someone else's field?"* Dysfunction is a danger indeed. YOU could be sick with COMPARISON, and not even know it. Especially when its behavior and actions feel natural to You.

LIFE'S MEANING will never be completely comprehended nor understood, when one's heart is clouded in DYSFUNCTION. Any form of AWAKENING, LIGHT, or REVELATION, will be deemed as judgmental, overwhelming, and destructive, especially when that LIGHT is exposed from the OUTSIDE *"instead from WITHIN!"* Inner-Light reveals, while outer Light *"blinds!"*

I presume it is safe to say, that we all realize *"our sources of Love,"* as it relates to our sources of personal confidence being, and worthiness. If we find these *"sources"* in friendships, that is where we will look. In family, this is where we will look. In companionships, this is where we will look. In careers, this is where we will look. In GOD, this is where we will look. I cannot make YOU *"seek"* where your desires are not. I cannot manipulate the cries of your soul. I cannot *"kidnap"* your perspectives in order to *"make you SEE!"*

Even though CHRIST IS THE ANSWER, Christ *"may not be one's individual Source of fulfillment!"* That will require an INNER LIIGHT to transition one's reality, and not an OUTER LIGHT that will blind the receiver!

My best version of existence and Being-ness will never be realized where it is obligated or forced. Wherever my life is obligated, resistance will be a reoccurring process and experience. My true wealth of life will be found where the Attraction draws my total surrender, as well as a continual yielding of who I perceive myself to be to my own self.

When God is seemingly being *"forced on me"* for an answer, I will fight back to maintain the control and familiar conveniences that seem to *"honor"* the *"ME"* that I know myself to be, to me.

TO THOSE and TO THEM...

"To those" serves as a major, identifying term that strategically, sets apart the classes of differences we are speaking of as it relates to SOURCES. **ROMANS 8:28** says, *"And we know that all things work together for the good OF THOSE (TO THEM) who LOVE GOD, to them who are the called, according to HIS purpose!*

Wherever our LOVE and STRENGH resides, YOU WILL FIND OUR GREATEST POWER! The nature, legality, and strength of our SOURCES, are determined by its capacity to last and endure TIME. If endurance means nothing to YOU, then you will settle for whatever your source of happiness provides YOU. We all become a reflection of the standards and powers of our Sources. The Divine Source states *that it makes one rich while adding "no sorrow with it,"* **PROVERBS 10:22, KJV.**

SOURCES IMPART THEIR LIFE CAPACITIES INTO THE RECEIVER..

Anxiety and Depression are byproducts of the Nature of what Source it is. Cycles are byproducts of the Nature of what Source it is. Whatever is the nature, determines the realities of the essence and energies of that source. We all, are the residue, seed, and reflection of the powers that our sources *"impart within us!"* In other words, I feel as *"what I am one with."* If the relationships you seek and find happiness in, are continually leaving you with anxiety, you may need to reassess its necessity! WISDOM says, It will not add sorrow to us. We manage to carry all the stresses, benefits, rewards, and longevities of the Sources we pursue.

To those, who seek career sources, "there are stresses, benefits, rewards, and longevities!"

To those, who seek family sources; the same. And on and on, regardless of what those *"sources"* may be. We become the natural expressions and patterns of the sources we seek. We become the realities and byproducts of those sources from which we find happiness.

Our behavior and actions serve as the offspring of those sources. The longevity of our happiness are the offspring of those sources. The stresses we manage, as well as the benefits we experience, are all offspring of the sources we pursue. We cannot cross-pollinate Sources. We cannot make a Kingdom Source *"collaborate with any other sources."* The Kingdom serves as its own. If we feel that we can mix up the sources, the *"source"* we are currently serving is confused. We all are the images and likeness of our pursuits.

I will not find my greatest power in anything that does not resonate my heart's desire. I will even find myself managing the stresses that occur within the parameters of my heart's desire. That is why an *"abusive relationship cannot be seen through the eyes of the victim that is experiencing it!"* They can manage the stress of the abuse when they find happiness with the person administrating it upon them!

We find our *"SUPERPOWER"* whenever we are in the Presence of our Source, regardless of what source is. Yet, how does that *"superpower"* leave us emotionally and spiritually? How does it leave us within the confines of confidence? Does your *"superpower"* lead you to comparison with others, or, does it leave YOU *"perfected, established, strengthened, and settled,* **I Peter 5:10, KJV.**

How does your superpower leave you resting? Sleeping? Providing? Thriving? Is your superpower *"temporary?"* Are you requiring miracles from your superpower? Wherever your Desires are, your Powers will be. Wherever your Love resides, your Powers and Abilities will be. Wherever your Source of being lives, so will YOU! We all reside within the culture of our Desires and Sources.

Even our personal growth and expansion captures the pace of our heart's desire. We all grow *"at the speed"* of our adoration. Our Source determines the powers, pace, and purpose of how we grow and mature. It reveals the pace and strength of the process from which we arise and awaken. Slow, to no growth occurs within unloved spaces. That growth, if any, will not and does not, bear any fruit which relates to that unloved environment. It will only grow frustration, as a result of tolerating a space that it will not personally enjoy. A *"hostaged heart"* will only plan and seek its escape from an atmosphere that has not adopted its source of life.

We are never tempted by what we despise. When we are tempted, we are tempted with the residue of what we already desire. When we perceive the Kingdom as something *"we are obligated to live,"* instead of a Source we are in love with and find our Superpower, we will continue to be tempted by an invitation of our *"suppressed love affair in another source,"* and we will reawaken to our inner turmoil. We can never be tempted by what we hate. If we are existing within a place of obligation, all of our senses to temptation will manifest. But, when we exist within the parameters of our sources of love, nothing will draw us out of it.

Distractions exist where our focus are mismanaged. Especially, when we are existing in spaces of indifference and absence of love. If we are existing within the realm of neediness and comparison, we will naturally *"invite"* ourselves into a new reality of space. When our existence is obligating and survival based, our soul will seek a space of escape. Remember what Solomon said, *"nothing new under the sun!"*

CHAPTER TWO
Where Are You "Living?

What we experience is determined by the space from which we exist. Are you living within the space that inspires your superpower? Or, are you existing where your survival requires you to be, in order to be provided for? Are you requiring *"the weekends"* in order to have a temporal access to your *"love spaces?"* Where do You live in the midst of the spaces your heart encounters daily? Do you sense that existing within the totality of your Source is even possible? Are you living in the Presence of the Spark that totally inspires your Superpower? That *"POWER"* is already within us, awakening to full degree when in the Presence of its Source of Being. Your greatest ability leaps when it's in the presence of its company and family. But when it is forced to be hidden and suppressed out of obligation, or in fear of being exposed to the *"wrong family,"* your emotions will fight you and blame you for taking your existence somewhere where it's not appreciated.

IN THE PRESENCE OF GOD, IS THE FULLNESS OF JOY!

....in thy Presence is fullness of JOY, **Psalm 16:11, KJV.** In the Presence of the Source *"of those who love the God-source,"* is FULLNESS OF JOY. It is not a temporal happiness and condition of the perfect elements aligning around me. In the PRESENCE of my SOURCE, is the fullness of JOY. My SUPERPOWER! In the presence of what my soul yearns for. In the Presence of MY LOVE and DESIRE, I find my greatest POWER! It is not found on a certain day, in a certain hour, when everything is right around me. I am always in the Presence of what I love most. I am always in the Presence of what I desire most. I AM POWER, always!

My life, rhythm, and schedule, are active practitioners of my SUPERPOWER. They will not lead me away from my most, powerful self and its ideals; just as *"your sources"* will not lead YOU away from its ideals. The issue is this, however. Why would someone's sources, leave them begging for more? Why would another source, leave you *"looking over the fence into someone else's yard?"*

You too, have experienced your *"best fun"* in the presence of those sources that give you life and meaning, regardless of its longevity.

16

Whatever your source is, will enable you to find pleasure in whatever benefits it provides you. We continue in relationships that benefit us, regardless of the stress they've caused us. Our loyalty is our testament to those things we have allowed within our spaces of pleasure. And if we have benefitted from it, we have also provided the grace that overlooked its need for perfection. Many can say the same about our relationships with GOD. We can perceive within ourselves, that all of our *"relationships"* are equally the same. And that is true.

It is about what we are willing to endure and stand. It is all based on our own heart, and not the comparison between various wills, gods, and promises. We are the images of what we are seeking after. GOD will be HIMSELF, regardless of the matter. Remember, there are *"THOSE, and THEMS!"* To THOSE, who love the Lord. We cannot speak of *"THOSE"* who love something else. Maybe, *"THEY"* can write a book of *"THEIR"* love space, grace, and places.

YOUR PLACE OF SUPERPOWER IS NOT COMPLEX..

Are you ashamed of where your *"power"*

awakens? Are you mingling in spaces that leave you ashamed? Why does your source allow you to mingle where shame will be experienced, or where you may even perceive yourself to be judged by the environment? Whenever you're in the Presence of what your Soul desires, your gifts will leap. Your best version will scream out loud. You will finally be YOU. We are only NOT WHO WE ARE, when in places of WHO WE ARE NOT! When we are trespassing, we become strangers. We become hypocrites!

Who you truly are awakens within desired spaces. Who you truly are is silent in the visitors' camp. It is not your home. We become servants and slaves in the territories of another. But we are offspring and family when we are home. This is not complex. We ALL ARE ALIVE WHEN WE ARE IN THE SPACE OF OUR IDENTITY. We become people in disguise when we are not, and after a while, we become burdened with playing a role, and we will need to get away in order to breathe!

If we cannot be, who we are being forever and consistently, then we are not existing at home. If who we are revealing to others, is not who we are truly, we will always live attached to other worlds and systems. The POWER in existing in your love space is this; YOU WILL NEVER HAVE TO CHANGE FOR ANYONE! The burdens and stresses that come with compromise will be long gone. If I cannot BE THE ME that I AM, why stress? Yet, why are YOU TRYING TO BE YOU *"in someone else's space?"* DO YOU TRULY KNOW WHO YOU ARE? In what space does YOUR POWER, thrive? Why are YOU trespassing?

When we are experiencing our divine alignment, we find ourselves empowered with the capacity to endure the stresses of our Alignment. We find ourselves continuing with the JOYS of our divine reality, regardless of the storms that arrive. Every system has a storm involved. Yet, the Power of that system is determined by how SURE WE ARE STANDING when it passes over!

The nature of who we are is authentically revealed, *"after the storms are over!"*

Your consistency abounds where your LOVE abounds. Are YOU ashamed of where it abounds? Your Powers should not leave

YOU feeling ashamed. We are only ashamed when we are trying to fool someone else into accepting us, validating us, or approving us. Are our sources leaving us feeling ashamed? If so, are our sources ashamed within themselves and denying themselves?

Is your power, *"super?"* Or, is it ashamed of itself and also ashamed of playing YOU against YOU? Imagine, establishing a life-long reality within your LOVE SPACE. Do you have faith enough in it? Do you perceive that it can, and will support YOU? Or, did you fall in *"love"* with the idea of someone else's space, and you're tormented within because you don't know if *"that space"* will allow you to live in it?

DO YOU KNOW WHERE YOU'RE SUPPOSED TO LIVE?

Are you currently on a hunt for the *"superpower"* spaces that are found in others? Are you *"house-hunting?"* Has your *"source"* left you out in the cold? Are you currently experiencing an *"abusive relationship?"* Yet, you've managed to tolerate the stress of it because it brings out a *"superpower"* within you that you can live with it? DYSFUNCTION *"functions so naturally,"* that one's Consciousness is not even aware that the Mind is diseased. It's almost impossible to evict one's self from its love space, regardless of the trauma. As stated earlier, UNLESS LIGHT IS REVEALED FROM WITHIN, it will blind and overwhelm one's eyes when experienced FROM WITHOUT! An awakening from WITHIN will go farther than awakening from WITHOUT. Saul, who became PAUL at his conversion on Damascus, experienced a LIGHT from the OUTSIDE, but He heard a VOICE FROM WITHIN! Those around him "saw the Light," but HE, *HEARD THE VOICE!"* **ACTS 9:3-4, KJV.**

Your inspired space of SUPERPOWER will never allow you to wander off. It is your source of existence and it will never *"turn off"* the Power in order to provoke You to *"search for water"* somewhere else. The Nature and Capacity of the Source is determined by the nature in which it provides for its benefactors. It will either leave you with sorrow, anxiety, depression, and loneliness. Or, it will feed your soul with STRENGHT, POWER, ENDURANCE, and MIGHT!

It's not found within the hardships it protects

You from, but in the sturdiness, you yet experience *"as a result of withstanding the storms"* in the NAME OF EVERYTHING YOU LOVE!

I naturally recognized my inner-power when in the Presence of my heart's desire. I even created a career from that very space. Got married and became a father from that space. Built my life and everything I AM from that space. Fell ill from that space. Remained alive, *in spite of,* from that space. Our greatest healing and wealth patterns are results of the space from which we find our superpower!

Again, it's hard to discover a power from a space that has yet to spark your heart. You can even say that *"I want that space to do something to me!"* And it will not. Your superpower is a natural, innate seed of CAUSE that is already residing within YOU! It is there by way of Spirit, or by way of comparison, by way of lust or by coveting someone else's fields. Or, by way of an emptiness which produces an inward need of significance. I don't know what your story is. But, I do know and recognize the source of cravings.

"FOR WHAT REASONS, DO YOU LOVE IT?"

Do you know why You want what You want? Do you know why YOU crave what it is YOU crave? No one can determine your longings but that thing that is being longed for, by YOU! In what ways *"is that missing thing"* valuable to You? Are you comparing someone else's thing and it's causing You to want *"your own thing,"* too? Have you determined the value of whatever is missing and have decided that you needed it too? As stated before, DYSFUNCTION acts so natural, that the mind can be diseased and have no clue of failure.

When we are ignorant of our own desires and reasons, the need to be like others, will become the fuel that ignites everything we do. Our source then becomes *"pleasing others,"* from which we find a myriad of *"superpowers"* when it comes to manipulating the room to recognize where we are, as well as our need for their companionship! We find ourselves continually doing good for others, while ever dying on the inside. Yet, we feel as though we cannot exist without pleasing others. Thus, finding ourselves suffering behind the need or lack of their validation of us. We find ourselves pleasing them in order to earn their approval. We become *"talented, gifted and empowered to please!"* Yet, we are without value and *"naked and ashamed"* within our own existence. THEIR NEEDS *"awaken our gifts,"* and we soon find THEM to be *"gods to us,"* while our ORIGINAL CREATOR IS DYING A SLOW DEATH WITHIN OUR CONSCIOUSNESS!

A source that has yet to settle its foundation of LOVE, as well as its settled-ness of need within the one who is engaged in a relationship with it. will never truly satisfy the soul. *"Am I truly loving what I'm loving?"* Or, am I *"loving the idea of a love that I desire to experience?"* *"Do I really know what LOVE is?"* *"Am I desiring to feel more accepted by someone my heart approves?"* "Have I approved myself, and by what Standards?" These are things that the Consciousness speaks at times, *"without it letting us know!"*

Yet, I cannot speak against the sources that inspire You. Everyone has a source of something that makes them feel the way they Desire. Everyone has a source that awakens, what they've considered to be, their *"power!"* And that particular power establishes the realities they desire to experience and depend on. They become ALIVE when in the Presence of the Spark that naturally reveals who they are *"in their world!"* We are all *"the images and likeness"* of the love of our own souls. Our strength wakes us when we are in the Presence of what we desire and love. And we all become weak when we are in a *"strange land!"*

IMAGINE...

Imagine working a career that is totally different from my Passion? Imagine the toleration, stress, and mismanagement that one would experience. Imagine an existence that is totally absent of a *"love seed;"* an existence that leaves us at the mercy of a loveless routine of survival and obligation. Imagine a survival that abandons us, and leaves us to the daily regulation of a loveless career. An existence, absent of LOVE, cannot help but compare itself to others, while seeking to FOLLOW AFTER THEM FOR COMPANIONSHIP, BUT NOT FOR TRANSFORMATION, NOR BECOMING!

Codependency becomes the *"superpower"* of the loveless and desire-less. To be empowered by one's need to be needed, and to develop a relationship in order to continually *"feel"* needed, becomes a natural norm. Can you imagine that? This reality becomes a constant *"nothing new under the sun!"* Therefore, we become addicted and expectant of life's *"constant loop"* in the cycle of life and humanity!

CHAPTER THREE
What's Missing? Can It Supply?

Where is my *"happy place"* or *"source of life,"* located? I will tell you. Imagine this; You are in the midst of a dead-end job. You constantly imagine walking out of the door because you're definitely tired of the cycle! *Where do you see yourself going in your heart? Is that "place" ready to receive YOU? If not, why?*

There is a *"source of survival"* wherewith we naturally find that it is responsible for regulating our entire lives. The source of having a job, even if we do not care for it, determines when and how we wake up every morning and go on our way. The obligation found behind maintaining important responsibilities, as well as the *"toils of living,"* determine our loyalties and commitment to something *"we have no desire to do!"*

We live, seeking to survive with the best of our ability, an existence that we do not love. The *"job"* is so much responsible for our daily living, that its demands and requirements can even *"call us away"* from a moment of Worship to fulfill its needs. Even while applying for *"survival,"* the job will require a, 1. Drug test 2. References

3. Educational references and academic sources 4. Capacity to be relocated or ability to work weekends.

The *"source of survival"* that we seek after, desires to commit the majority of our entire lives, to a 40-50 hour work week, to secure the promise of a paycheck that will enable us to continue on with our survival. This is not a slap against work. Work is essential.

The question is, have YOU properly defined the *"source of your greatest power,"* to the *"source of your obligation and survival?"* When LOVE is defined, can we too, exist from the source of our wealth passions? For *"mere survival"* we will give up our entirety of living in exchange for *"2 weeks of relief!"*

Again, this is nothing against the reality of Work. But *"what kind of work?"* Is it based on a *"love-less"* existence? Or, an obligatory existence that destroys the gifts, callings, and purposes in one's life?

David killed his giants "from the realm of the Presence" from which he found his joy and "superpower!" It was from this reality that he protected his fathers' flocks; experienced his wins against wild animals, lions, and bears; killed Goliath, as well as his "tens of thousands," and obtained the throne!

He carried "this Source" within him, to the point that it totally maintained his daily supply and life source. He lived his life's schedule, as well as established the daily events in his life, FROM THIS SOURCE OF GREAT JOY! From the Presence of GOD, his daily reality was formed and lived out. The fullness of JOY planned out his day and was revealed from the Manifestation of Presence within his core being.

I wonder what is the "missing link" from totally existing from that particular "source and presence" that is responsible for us living our best lives? What's the secret, "if there is a secret?"

Are we existing from an obligation instead of the presence which produces our superpower? What are we not doing or applying, where our superpower is not serving as the source of our existence? Why isn't the source of my superpower, not the active and legal supplier of my daily life? Is my superpower merely temporary, fleeting emotions and ideas?

We will naturally function FOR THE SUPPLIER of the source. If people pleasing provided the source, we will function for them. If GOD provided it, we will function for HIM. Whatever "the cause" that inspired the power, will determine one's longevity and confidence with living and manifesting the power. This is what reveals and determines the Purpose.

What are we missing? Is it a certain Discipline and Focus? Can the "presence" that activates our power, sustain us daily? Why can't we surrender to it? Is that space "real?" Can we yield ourselves to it in the same manner that we surrender ourselves to our places of employment? Maybe inwardly, we have a "sense in knowing the circumstances" that are responsible for producing "those special powers that we have no confidence nor conviction in. It is close to impossible to surrender our entire existence to codependent forms of energy and trauma, as well as gifts that were birthed from a "flawed, people source" and "people pleasing!" We innately know that to continue in that particular power, that sense of Dysfunction must remain fueled by certain people, places, and things. This mindset will be forever joined to another individual, and the ability to break free from them will be non-existent.

Yet, when the power is birthed through an Eternal Source, the confidence to "allow" oneself to be sustained, will be more natural and willing. Our levels of faith are determined by the realities that are responsible for that faith. We are as confident, courageous, and resilient as the circumstances that are responsible for that source. The nature of the source "determines our capacity" within the source.

There is a "sphere" within us all, that knows and reveals everything. So, the question would be, "How can I willfully ignore the essence of MY BEST VERSION OF SELF, and connect it to a place of toil?" Is MY BEST VERSION OF SELF a mere hobby? What discipline am I ignoring from the realities of my superpowers? Is my power only super, when it is free of responsibility? Am I seeking to hide from the presence of other people? Am I fearing accountability with my power? Am I afraid to be seen with it? Am I only "super" in the dark?

Why have this power "if it is afraid of making a way" for Me? Did I "steal" the idea from someone else? Am I pretending with it? It would be hard to release myself to a pretense, right? Am I simply carrying with me "the presence of another person" in order to be validated by the essence of the person "that I seek to carry within me?" If my "power" is from another, then WHO AM I? (What's amazing is this; my Life will not release Me to fully be supported by What I Am Not).

My greatest version of Myself, will always find itself awakened within the Presence of my heart's desire, regardless of the quality of that desire. And when I am in the presence of the core that is responsible for it, there will be a shift in my personal capacity. Once again, the "presence of that joy" can be carried within. But, if that presence is held hostage within a certain space, person, or time schedule, is it truly a source? Or, is it a mere moment that must be continually manipulated in order to fulfill?

This Divine Source that I am personally, as well as experientially referring to, is the KINGDOM. As I stated earlier, Christ is the Answer to EVERYTHING, yet He may not be the Source for everyone's "greatest happiness and superpower." This Reality is based on one's core sense of being, and value. The Source that I am familiar with, placed the CORE of my Power within Me.

When I did not yet Value my Reality, whenever I looked within Myself, I found "something," but I did not find "THAT THING!" Whenever we are not in love with WHO, WHAT, and WHY we are, we will continually perceive the goods in another, but not ourselves.

Whenever GOD provides us with a treasure of Wisdom, and we do not perceive its value, we will have a sense of GOD is "providing us with nothing," instead of providing us with SOURCE! When true love is despised, we will hate the fact that we must overly rethink everything from GOD instead of simply "receiving the fulfilling-ness of what we requested!"

Can GOD honor my request, please? In plain English? In Black and White? Why must it be so complex?

The Wisdom of the Divine Source has always provided our quickening power and storehouse of Treasure/ The issue has been that His ways are not always valued. The "sources" of our truest happiness, and not the Sources that we feel "obligated to honor," will always tell us Who those "particular presents" were sent by. It will also make us aware if those presents are what we actually desired! When the heart feels "obligated" in honoring a source that is not responsible for its innate desire, it becomes impossible to "see" the value in that gift. Esau did not see the value of his birthright, simply because his desire for food in his moment of hunger, was greater than the Destiny that was assigned for him; **Genesis 25:29-34, KIV.**

A non-valued Source will not sustain, not because it is not powerful enough, but because its Strength is not what the moment is desiring! Esau said, "I am about to die, what good is the birthright to Me?", **Genesis 25:32, KJV.**

David existed from the realms of the Presence that was responsible for his Strength, Wisdom, and Capacity. I call it, SUPERPOWER. He lived his daily reality from this Truth. He lived his Kingship from this reality. He lived his humanity from this reality. He was even restored from his faults, sins, and personal detours from this reality! The Source empowered him, and it also delivered him!

Whatever *"source"* we are utilizing, have you ever took the time to notice the particular traits it leaves with us? Has it provided us with confidence and assurance? Or, does it lead us to others for that? The nature of a source is determined by how well we survive from it. Is it leaving us hungry, and needing others to lift us up? Is the source *"dependent"* oriented? Can it provide for me? Or, does it empower Me with the capacity to believe in Myself to the fullest?

WHAT CAN YOU TOLERATE?

The love we have for a thing, determines the nature of the endurance we also have with that thing. Love determines one's endurance within a Covenant Relationship and Pattern. It determines the patience and power from which I can survive a *"serious blow"* in life. I will either tolerate it because I am afraid of a future that I am not prepared to face. Or, I will endure it because I strategically discern that this Path is an intricate part of my divine destiny. As I tolerate it, I maintain my fears of responsibility and true growth. I will find myself sitting in the same place as years before. Same conversation. Forever learning, but never coming to a significant conclusion.

Yet, when I endure the Process out of true love, I BECOME AN IMAGE of the love that I am loving with. I become something as powerful as the Process itself. Toleration and Endurance, are entirely different Powers! A tolerated marriage leads to adultery and detours. But an endured Covenant *"leads to greater vision and purposes!"*

Covenants lead to either Generational Powers, or divorce. Covenants reveal whether or not the *"courtship and engagement"* were lies, or Truths. Covenants reveal who we truly are, and not just who we presented ourselves to be in order to be approved and accepted.

In a fairy-tale world, we can find ourselves treating our courtship as though it were Covenant. We are in love with the idea of love. Yet, time and promises spoken, reveal everything.

Can YOU tolerate living from *"that source that is responsible for your personal happiness?"* Or, is it an escape option? You can believe that whatever Wisdom has provided as our Source in experiencing our Greatest Version of Self, it can definitely be lived from for everything.

It's not about being labeled as *"self-employed,"* but about being empowered from a reality of SELF IN-LOVED! Many lack the disciplines of being their own boss, even though they're creative and gifted. Many lack the logistics of business, even if they can perform certain duties.

But tragically, when we are absent of BEING IN LOVE WITH OUR DIVINE DESIGN, we possess no capacity to even live from ourselves. The Divine Source loses it capacity to carry us, when we have also despised carrying it within ourselves.

CHAPTER FOUR
Where Is That "Space," Again?

Answer these Questions truthfully. You are not obligated to place *"God, or religion"* in your answers. Speak the Truth to Yourself.

Where do You feel your Greatest Power and Joy?

Where are You your happiest?

In what Atmosphere do You feel the most freeing?

In what Atmosphere do You feel no shame?

When do You feel your most Mature and full of Wisdom?

What places or realms, do You love and desire most?

Have You defined a Hope and Reality from which You can live, continually?

Wherever Love and Desire resides, our greatest strength, joy, and power will be revealed. We become, wherever we truly desire to BE. It cannot be learned. It simply comes alive when we are there.

True Covenant Love will empower us to commit to the Very End, *even BEFORE the Journey ever begins.*

So, what's keeping YOU from having it?

"Living from your Vision definitely requires Discipline and Responsibility. You must first find HONOR in your own Voice, if you're going to work from your Voice."

We are the natural representatives, ambassadors, and ministers of those things that naturally awaken our most prominent and fluid selves. And regardless of its quality, nature, or type, We find it hard to break away from what it is. We are the Image of what it is, as well as Who it is. When others *"see"* YOU, they also *"see"* that Thing that inspires YOU!

Many of us have lived such judgmental and existences of comparison, that our conscience and ability to critically think, are severely clogged with indecision. They are definitely living from a certain Source, and may not yet perceive it. They have yet to realize that

"those particular spaces" where they feel
from judgment, demands, and comparison,
are really *their "happy spaces!" And they are
tolerating their limited longevity.*

"I'll leave You with This!"

Every individual is responsible for the realities
of their own happiness, fulfillment, and joy. We
are not required to judge anyone, or diminish
anyone for being motivated and encouraged
through their *"rightful concept"* to whatever
means or source that they desire.

Yet, the issue comes by way of complaint,
dissatisfaction, and un-fulfillment. Do YOU
have a desire to experience an *"everlasting
power, confidence, and assurance of Being?"*
Do YOU have a yearning to experience a
continual stream of Creativity, Excellence,
and Significance that can endure any season
of Turmoil? Are you seeking for a personal
power that will maintain a Discipline that will
yet carry YOU through, even when Motivation
may be absent?

Well, are YOU realizing these qualities within
your current realm of *"happiness?"* Have
you determined the *"terms, as well as the deal*

breakers," for YOU obtaining it? How far will YOU go? How much are YOU willing to invest to realize it?

"The kingdom is like a treasure hidden in a field. When a man found it, he hid it again, and then IN HIS JOY, went a sold all that he had, and bought THAT field," **Matthew 13:44. KJV.**

That Source is the ONE THING that would inspire YOU to EXCHANGE EVERYTHING for the WHOLE THING! Some sources motivate us to do absolutely nothing. And if we feel our best, while doing nothing, then "nothing" is what we deserve. No judgment nor condemnation, here.

If we feel our best, while hidden in the dark, while far, far away from the world's troubles; then we will remain invisible to the rest of the world. The choice is yours. Enjoy your invisibility to the fullest.

But do not complain, belittle, and discriminate against those whose LIGHT are awakening the Planet to a New Possibility. Do not spread or contaminate other sources *"will vial judgments that are the byproducts of temporary joy spaces that have burned themselves out!"*

From your place of Source, have YOU realized the Christ that YOU are, *"or, are you yet the person that you're trying to maintain on your terms?"*

www.ingramcontent.com/pod-product-compliance
Lightning Source LLC
Chambersburg PA
CBHW070341290526
45791CB00003B/1429